Essential HVAC Troubleshooting; A Technician's Handbook

Dutch Pearson

Table of Contents

chapter 1

Understanding Digital Gauge Readings nderstanding digital gauge readings is essential for HVAC technicians to accurately diagnose and maintain systems. Reading these metrics allows technicians to identify issues early, ensuring efficient performance and prolonging the lifespan of HVAC equipment. This chapter will equip readers with the skills necessary to interpret digital gauge data effectively.

Throughout this chapter, we will cover key metrics displayed on digital gauges, including suction and discharge pressure readings, temperature differentials, and flow rates. These metrics are vital for assessing system health and diagnosing problems such as refrigerant charge issues, airflow problems, and potential blockages. Additionally, we will discuss common errors in reading digital gauges, emphasizing the importance of accurate measurements and the influence of environmental factors. By understanding these aspects, technicians can improve their diagnostic accuracy and enhance system reliability.

Dutch Pearson

Key Metrics on Digital Gauges

Understanding the various metrics displayed on digital gauges is fundamental for HVAC technicians. Accurate interpretations of these readings can significantly impact diagnostic precision and efficient system performance assessments. Let's delve into the essential metrics and their relevance to HVAC diagnostics.

Suction and discharge pressure readings are critical components in diagnosing refrigerant charge issues and overall system efficiency. Suction pressure, measured at the low side of the system, provides insight into the evaporator's operations. If this pressure is too high or low, it indicates potential problems such as an overcharged or undercharged system, respectively. Discharge pressure is recorded on the high side of the system and affects how efficiently the refrigerant is being condensed and moved out of the compressor. Elevated discharge pressure could indicate a dirty condenser coil or an obstruction in the refrigeration pathway, while low discharge pressure may signal a leak or insufficient refrigerant. Understanding these pressures and knowing what constitutes normal ranges aid in identifying potential failures early, preventing major breakdowns.

Temperature differentials are equally significant for troubleshooting airflow problems and diagnosing coil issues. Temperature readings allow technicians to recognize conditions that affect the evaporator and condenser coils. Superheat, the temperature above boiling point when all liquid has turned to vapor, helps in assessing if enough refrigerant is entering the evaporator. Insufficient superheat can result in liquid refrigerant returning to the compressor, which may cause severe damage. On the other hand, subcooling measures the temperature below the condensing point where liquid refrigerant is fully condensed. Proper subcooling ensures that the refrigerant is completely liquefied, avoiding gas bubbles that can hinder cooling effectiveness. By understanding these calculations, technicians can enhance service accuracy and optimize system performance.

Monitoring flow rates for refrigerants or air is another crucial aspect for maintaining system efficiency. Digital gauges typically display flow metrics, indicating the volume and speed of refrigerants or air passing through the system. Deviations from normal flow rates can alert technicians to blockages or inefficiencies within the system. For instance, a decrease in refrigerant flow could suggest a clogged filter dryer or partial blockage in the expansion valve. Similarly, abnormal air flow rates might indicate restrictions in the ductwork or dirty filters. Regular monitoring of these metrics ensures optimal system performance and enables technicians to perform proactive maintenance, thus extending the equipment's life.

Modern digital gauges often come equipped with built-in diagnostic alerts. These features notify technicians of system irregularities that require immediate attention. Alerts can range from indicating high or low-pressure conditions to more advanced notifications about potential electrical faults or sensor malfunctions. Familiarity with these alerts allows technicians to swiftly respond to issues before they escalate, enhancing service reliability and reducing downtime for clients. For example, a real-time alert about rising discharge pressure can prompt a technician to immediately inspect and clean the condenser coil before it leads to a compressor failure.

Common Errors in Gauge Readings

Identifying and avoiding common mistakes in reading digital HVAC gauge data is crucial for accurate diagnostics and effective system maintenance. This subpoint focuses on key areas where errors often occur and provides clear guidelines to help technicians improve their accuracy and reliability.

Misreading pressure units, such as confusing PSI with other measurements, is a prevalent issue that can lead to significant diagnostic errors. For instance, PSI (pounds per square inch) is commonly used in the United States, whereas other regions might use kilopascals (kPa) or bar. Misinterpreting these units can result in incorrect assessments of system health. Technicians must be adept at unit conversion to ensure consistency and accuracy, particularly when working in a global context where different standards may apply. Understanding these conversions and applying them correctly can dramatically enhance the reliability of a technician's readings, ultimately leading to more accurate diagnostics and better system performance.

Environmental factors play a significant role in affecting gauge readings. Ambient temperature, for instance, can skew the results obtained from digital gauges. If the surrounding temperature is significantly different from the standard operating conditions, it can impact the pressure readings. For example, during a hot summer day, the ambient heat could cause an increase in pressure readings. Conversely, colder temperatures might show lower pressure readings than actual. Technicians should be aware of these environmental influences and make necessary adjustments to compensate for temperature variations. This awareness ensures that the diagnostics performed are valid and reflect the true state of the HVAC system, leading to more precise troubleshooting and maintenance.

Regular calibration of gauges is another critical aspect that must not be overlooked. Over time, even the most reliable digital gauges can drift from their calibrated settings due to wear and tear or environmental factors. This drift can introduce errors in readings, misleading troubleshooting efforts. Establishing a consistent calibration schedule is essential to maintaining the accuracy of these instruments. Regular calibration checks should be part of a technician's routine, ensuring that the gauges provide correct data each time they are used. By adhering to a set calibration schedule, technicians can avoid the pitfalls of inaccurate readings and contribute to the overall safety and efficiency of the HVAC systems they maintain.

Each HVAC system operates under specific conditions unique to its design and location. Recognizing these system-specific parameters is vital for accurate gauge readings. For example, older systems might have different pressure ranges compared to newer, more efficient models. Similarly, systems designed for industrial applications may operate under different conditions than those meant for residential use. A technician must understand these unique requirements and how they impact gauge readings. Ignoring these nuances can lead to incorrect service conclusions, potentially causing further issues rather than solving existing ones. By taking into account the specific conditions of each system, technicians can make informed decisions that align with the system's operational needs and ensure optimal performance.

Summary and Reflections

In this chapter, we have explored the critical role of accurately reading and interpreting digital gauge data in HVAC diagnostics. By understanding suction and discharge pressures, technicians can diagnose refrigerant charge issues and overall system efficiency. Temperature differentials, such as superheat and subcooling, offer insights into the evaporator and condenser coil conditions, aiding in precise troubleshooting. Monitoring flow rates for refrigerants or air helps identify blockages or inefficiencies within the system, while built-in diagnostic alerts on modern gauges allow for swift responses to irregularities.

We also highlighted common errors that can occur when reading digital HVAC gauge data and ways to avoid them. Misreading pressure units, environmental factors affecting gauge readings, and the necessity for regular calibration are all crucial points addressed. Recognizing the unique parameters of each HVAC system ensures accurate gauge readings and effective maintenance. Armed with these skills and knowledge, technicians are better equipped to ensure optimal system performance and longevity, ultimately providing reliable service to their clients.

Reference List

Amazon.com . (2014). Amazon.com. https://www.amazon.com/CMTOOL-Digital-ManometerPressure-Tester/dp/B0C9J9C6F8

Amazon.com . (2014). Amazon.com. https://www.amazon.com/Digital-Manometer-DifferentialPressure-Gauge/dp/B0CDCM9TLC

Mastering HVAC Manifold Gauges: A Comprehensive Guide . (2023, October 25). Dowd Heat and Air | Your Tulsa HVAC Company. https://dowdheatandair.com/blog/mastering-hvacmanifold-gauges-a-comprehensive-guide/

admin. (2022, February 15). *How to Select a Pressure Gauge* . Reotemp Instruments. https://reotemp.com/products/pressure-gauges/how-to-select-a-pressuregauge/

chapter 2

Distinguishing Between TXV and Piston Systems

Distinguishing between TXV and piston systems is a fundamental skill for HVAC technicians. By accurately identifying these systems, professionals can ensure proper maintenance and troubleshooting processes, enhancing the efficiency and reliability of HVAC units. This chapter provides an instructive guide on recognizing the visual indicators and performance traits that differentiate TXV systems from piston systems.

The chapter begins by exploring the unique components of TXV systems, including the thermal expansion valve, sensing bulb, and adjustable superheat settings. It highlights key visual markers such as the brass body of the TXV, the presence of a power head connected to a capillary tube, and the location of the sensing bulb on the evaporator coil.

The content delves into the operational characteristics of TXV systems, emphasizing their dynamic response to varying loads and the importance of accurate superheat adjustments. Subsequently, the focus shifts to piston systems, detailing the fixed orifice design and the absence of expansion valves as primary identifiers.

Readers will learn about the placement of orifices in the condenser and the non-adjustable nature of superheat settings in piston systems. Through clear descriptions and practical guidelines, this chapter equips HVAC technicians with the knowledge needed to distinguish between these two prevalent types of refrigeration systems.

Visual identifiers of TXV systems

Accurate diagnostics and system identification are pivotal in the HVAC industry. One key method to achieve this is by recognizing the distinctive visual features of a Thermal Expansion Valve (TXV) system. TXV systems present several unique components and characteristics that make them identifiable and functional.

The most noticeable external component of a TXV system is the thermal expansion valve itself, which is typically mounted on the liquid line. This valve plays an essential role in regulating the refrigerant flow into the evaporator. Its position in the system layout makes it fairly easy to spot. In contrast to other systems, the TXV has a brass body with an inlet and an outlet valve. The configuration usually includes a removable cap designed for superheat adjustment. Often seen adjacent to the valve assembly is a power head connected to a capillary tube, which extends to a sensing bulb attached to the evaporator coil.

The sensing bulb location is another critical visual feature of a TXV system. This sensing bulb is firmly attached to the evaporator through copper tubing. The purpose of this bulb is to detect the temperature changes at the outlet of the evaporator. By being in direct contact with the pipe, the bulb ensures accurate measurement of the refrigerant temperature, facilitating efficient system control. The placement of the sensing bulb can vary, but it is typically found near the end of the evaporator coil, making it accessible for inspection and maintenance.

Guidelines for identifying the sensing bulb include looking for a small, cylindrical component wrapped around the evaporator outlet pipe with copper or stainless-steel tubing connecting it back to the TXV. The bulb should be securely fastened to ensure proper thermal contact and should be insulated to prevent false readings due to ambient temperature fluctuations.

Adjustment capabilities mark another distinguishing feature of TXV systems. Unlike fixed orifice systems, TXVs offer adjustable superheat settings. This adjustability allows technicians to finely tune the system for optimal performance, thereby enhancing energy efficiency and reliability. The superheat setting can be adjusted by removing the cap on the TXV and turning the adjustment screw, which alters the spring pressure inside the valve. This capability is particularly beneficial in environments where cooling loads fluctuate frequently, as it helps maintain consistent evaporator performance and avoids compressor issues such as slugging.

For accurate adjustment, follow these guidelines:

1. Measure the actual superheat level usingappropriate tools.

2. Adjust the TXV's adjustment screw in smallincrements, typically ¼ turn at a time.

3. Re-check the superheat after each adjustment toensure the desired setting is achieved.

4. Ensure the cap is replaced securely afteradjustments to protect the internal components.

TXV systems also exhibit specific behavior under varying loads. These systems are engineered to dynamically respond to load changes, adjusting the refrigerant flow accordingly. When the cooling load increases, the temperature at the evaporator outlet rises, causing the refrigerant inside the sensing bulb to expand and increase pressure. This pressure forces the diaphragm within the TXV to open wider, allowing more refrigerant to flow into the evaporator. Consequently, the superheat decreases, stabilizing the system's performance. Conversely, when the cooling load decreases, the process reverses, with the valve reducing the refrigerant flow to maintain optimal superheat levels.

This dynamic response ensures that the TXV system operates efficiently under different conditions, maintaining comfort levels and preventing energy wastage. For example, in commercial buildings where occupancy and heat loads can change throughout the day, TXVs adapt to these variations seamlessly, ensuring the HVAC system remains effective without manual intervention.

Understanding these visual and functional characteristics of TXV systems empowers HVAC technicians to make accurate diagnostics and system identifications. Recognizing a TXV system involves inspecting the liquid line for the thermal expansion valve, locating the sensing bulb attached to the evaporator, and identifying the adjustable superheat mechanism. Additionally, observing the system's behavior under varied loads provides further confirmation of its type.

Visual identifiers of piston systems

Understanding the distinctions between TXV and piston systems is fundamental for HVAC technicians. This subpoint focuses on identifying piston systems through their visual markers and performance traits, which are unique and distinguishable. By familiarizing oneself with these aspects, a technician can ensure accurate diagnostics and proper maintenance procedures.

Piston type components form the backbone of this system. Unlike TXVs (Thermostatic Expansion Valves), piston systems employ a fixed orifice design. This means that they do not possess an expansion valve, which is a key identifier. The fixed orifice design of a piston system allows a specific quantity of refrigerant to flow based on the system's operating conditions. These systems are typically simpler in construction compared to TXVs, resulting in fewer mechanical components and less potential for part failures. When inspecting the system, look for the absence of a thermal expansion valve, which is a clear indicator of a piston system. Instead, you will find a fixed orifice within the refrigeration circuit.

Guidelines for identifying piston type components involve looking for signs of a fixed orifice design. Check if the system lacks an expansion valve and, instead, has a small brass or copper component where the metering device should be. This simple design is the foremost visual hallmark distinguishing piston systems from other types. Equipped with this knowledge, a technician can quickly determine the presence of a piston system and proceed with relevant diagnostic steps.

The orifice placement within piston systems further differentiates them from TXVs. In piston systems, the orifices are located in the condenser, making them inaccessible in the same manner as TXVs. The placement of these orifices is crucial because it directly influences the system's performance. To identify this feature, inspect the condenser unit; you'll find there are no external adjustments or accessible parts for altering the orifice size. This contrasts starkly with TXV systems, where the expansion valve is often externally mounted and can be adjusted or replaced relatively easily. The concealed nature of the orifice in piston systems necessitates a different approach during maintenance and troubleshooting, often requiring more invasive inspection techniques.

Superheat settings present another identifiable trait. Piston systems do not have adjustable superheat controls. Superheat refers to the temperature increase of the refrigerant vapor above its boiling point once it is in a gaseous state. In TXV systems, the superheat can be finely tuned using the expansion valve, which dynamically adjusts the refrigerant flow based on load conditions. However, in piston systems, such dynamic adjustment is absent because the fixed orifice dictates a constant refrigerant flow rate. This results in a fixed superheat setting depending on the system design and operational parameters. Technicians can use this nonadjustability as a diagnostic clue: if the system appears to lack mechanisms for superheat adjustment, it is likely a piston system.

Understanding this characteristic assists technicians in recognizing and adapting their troubleshooting methods to accommodate the inherent design limitations of piston systems.

Performance characteristics of piston systems also provide insights into their identification. Piston systems tend to exhibit a more straightforward performance curve compared to TXVs. This simplicity manifests in predictable operational behavior under varying load conditions. TXVs adjust the refrigerant flow dynamically, leading to a variable performance curve that optimizes efficiency across different conditions. Conversely, piston systems maintain a steady performance without such dynamic adjustments. For instance, when a piston system experiences a sudden change in cooling demand, the fixed orifice continues to meter refrigerant at a constant rate, which may lead to less optimized performance temporarily. This straightforward behavior can be observed through consistent superheat levels and a more linear relationship between ambient temperature changes and system performance.

In practice, the identification process involves observing the system's response to load variations. A technician familiar with both TXV and piston systems should note how a system reacts when cooling demands fluctuate. Piston systems, given their nonadjustable nature, will show a less responsive adjustment in refrigerant flow compared to TXVs.

This characteristic performance gives away the system type and guides the technician towards appropriate maintenance strategies tailored to the specific system dynamics.

To summarize, recognizing piston systems involves looking for certain distinctive markers. The absence of an expansion valve and the presence of a fixed orifice design are primary indicators. Inspecting the condenser for the orifice placement reveals another telltale sign, emphasizing the need for internal checks rather than external adjustments. The nonadjustability of superheat settings further confirms the identification, highlighting the system's inherent simplicity. Finally, observing the system's straightforward performance curve provides additional clues.

Final Thoughts

In this chapter, we have explored the key visual identifiers that distinguish TXV and piston systems. For TXV systems, the presence of a thermal expansion valve on the liquid line, along with the sensing bulb attached to the evaporator, are primary markers. Additionally, the ability to adjust superheat settings provides further confirmation of a TXV system. On the other hand, piston systems can be identified by their fixed orifice design and the absence of an expansion valve. The simplicity of piston systems is reflected in their straightforward performance curves and steady refrigerant flow.

By understanding these visual and functional characteristics, HVAC technicians can accurately diagnose whether a system utilizes a TXV or piston approach. Recognizing these differences is vital for conducting proper maintenance and ensuring efficient operation. This knowledge empowers technicians to make informed decisions, adapt their troubleshooting methods accordingly, and optimize system performance based on the specific type of refrigeration system they encounter.

Reference List

NOCTI and Nocti Business Solutions (NBS) | NCCRS . (2020). Nationalccrs.org. https:// www.nationalccrs.org/organizations/nocti-and-noctibusiness

Pearson, A. (2005). *Carbon dioxide - New uses for an old refrigerant* . *International Journal of Refrigeration* , 28(8), 1140-1148. https://doi.org/ 10.1016/j.ijrefrig.2005.09.005

The Thermal Expansion Valve (TXV) Explained | United CoolAir . (2019, July 3). https:// www.unitedcoolair.com/the-thermal-expansionvalve-txv/

What Does A TXV Do? | 3 Important Benefits Of A TXV . (2023, April 7). The AC Therapist. https://theactherapist.com/blog/what-does-a-txv-do/

chapter 3

Diagnosing TXV vs Piston Systems Using Gauges

Diagnosing TXV vs Piston systems using gauges requires a keen understanding of their distinct operational characteristics. In HVAC systems, determining whether a Thermal Expansion Valve (TXV) or a piston is in use is fundamental to effective troubleshooting and system performance assessment. Each method of refrigerant control presents unique challenges and diagnostic indicators that can be accurately interpreted through the use of digital gauges. By grasping the core principles behind these two systems, technicians can enhance their diagnostic accuracy and optimize system functionality.

This chapter will explore specific techniques for analyzing gauge readings in both TXV and piston systems. For TXV systems, the chapter will delve into pressure differential analysis, temperature-pressure relationships, superheat calculations, and common symptoms identified through gauge readings. Additionally, it will cover static pressure measurements, fixed refrigerant flow characteristics, subcooling analysis, and potential problems indicated by gauge readings in piston systems. The aim is to equip HVAC technicians with practical knowledge and tools to distinguish between these systems efficiently, ensuring accurate diagnoses and effective resolutions.

Gauge Readings for TXV Systems

Analyzing gauge readings specific to TXV systems is crucial for HVAC technicians to diagnose and resolve issues effectively. This section provides insights into the pressure differential analysis, temperaturepressure relationship, superheat calculation, and common TXV symptoms.

Pressure Differential Analysis:
In TXV systems, the pressure differential between the low and high sides is a key indicator of system performance. Unlike fixed orifice systems, TXVs actively adjust to maintain optimal conditions, resulting in distinct pressure behaviors. In a properly functioning TXV system, the high side (discharge) pressure should be significantly higher than the low side (suction) pressure, reflecting effective refrigerant control across the evaporator coil. Understanding this differential helps technicians identify whether the TXV is modulating correctly or if there are potential blockages or leaks. For example, a narrower pressure

differential might indicate an underperforming TXV or insufficient refrigerant charge.

Temperature-Pressure Relationship:

Gauging the temperature-pressure relationship is another critical aspect of diagnosing TXV systems. The relationship between these two variables can reveal much about the system's operational status. To assess this, technicians need to measure both the temperature and pressure at various points within the system, specifically at the evaporator and condenser. A useful guideline to remember is that as the temperature in the evaporator rises, the corresponding pressure should also increase proportionally. If there's a discrepancy in this relationship, it could point to issues such as a malfunctioning TXV, improper refrigerant levels, or airflow problems (Tomczyk, 2018).

A practical approach involves comparing the measured values with standard charts or tables specific to the refrigerant type being used. These reference materials provide the expected pressure for a given temperature, allowing technicians to quickly identify anomalies. For example, if the evaporator temperature is 40°F, the corresponding pressure for R-410A refrigerant should be around 118 psi. Deviations from these norms necessitate further investigation into potential causes.

Superheat Calculation:

Superheat is a critical parameter in evaluating TXV performance. Superheat refers to the temperature difference between the refrigerant vapor exiting the evaporator and its saturation temperature. Proper superheat levels ensure that only vapor enters the compressor, preventing liquid refrigerant from causing damage. To calculate superheat, measure the suction line temperature at the evaporator outlet and subtract the saturation temperature (corresponding to the suction pressure).

For instance, if the suction line temperature is 55°F and the saturation temperature is 45°F, the superheat would be 10°F. Typically, a TXV system should maintain a superheat of around 10-15°F. Any deviation from this range suggests potential issues. Low superheat indicates excessive refrigerant flow, possibly due to an oversized or stuck-open TXV, whereas high superheat suggests insufficient refrigerant, which might be caused by a restricted or undercharged system.

Understanding superheat's significance extends beyond protecting the compressor; it also reflects the load on the evaporator. When an evaporator experiences varying heat loads, the TXV adjusts to stabilize superheat, ensuring efficient operation. For example, during lower load conditions, the TXV will partially close to maintain the desired superheat, highlighting its responsiveness compared to fixed orifice systems (Orr, 2020).

Common TXV Symptoms:

Recognizing typical symptoms through gauge readings is pivotal for diagnosing TXV-related problems. Common indicators include fluctuating pressures, inconsistent superheat, and abnormal temperature differentials. For instance, if the highside pressure is excessively high while the low-side pressure remains low, it might indicate a blocked TXV or a restriction in the liquid line.

Additionally, variations in superheat readings can signal TXV malfunctions. Low superheat often points to a valve stuck open or an oversized TXV, leading to excessive refrigerant flow and potential compressor flooding. Conversely, high superheat may result from a restricted TXV or low refrigerant charge, causing inadequate cooling and compressor overheating.

Another symptom is erratic or unstable pressure readings, which can reflect improper TXV modulation or system contamination. For instance, debris or contaminants obstructing the TXV can cause pressure surges and drops, making it challenging to maintain consistent operating conditions. Additionally, unequal temperature distribution across the evaporator coil can indicate TXV issues. If parts of the coil are significantly colder than others, it could suggest uneven refrigerant distribution, a sign of a failing or improperly adjusted TXV.

It's essential for technicians to consider these symptoms in context, conducting comprehensive inspections to pinpoint the exact cause of the problem. For example, if all signs point to a malfunctioning TXV but the system also exhibits low refrigerant levels, addressing both issues is necessary for effective resolution.

Gauge Readings for Piston Systems

In HVAC diagnostics, accurately determining whether a system uses a Thermal Expansion Valve (TXV) or a piston is fundamental. This section focuses specifically on piston systems, providing distinct gauge readings and diagnostic techniques.

Static Pressure Measurements

In piston systems, static pressure refers to the pressure within the refrigerant lines when the system is off. These measurements are essential as they help establish a baseline for system performance. Typically, piston systems display a more consistent static pressure compared to TXV systems, which exhibit variations due to their throttling characteristics. Technicians should measure static pressure first thing in the diagnostic process because it can highlight significant issues like refrigerant overcharge or undercharge. Always ensure that the system has been off long enough for pressures to equalize before taking these readings.

Fixed Refrigerant Flow

Piston systems operate with a fixed orifice, meaning the amount of refrigerant flow through the system is constant once the piston size is determined at installation. This characteristic significantly impacts the system's performance and how technicians should interpret gauge readings.

Guideline: Understanding fixed refrigerant flow helps in diagnosing issues such as improper piston sizing. An oversized piston will allow too much refrigerant flow, leading to lower suction pressure and higher superheat. Conversely, an undersized piston restricts refrigerant, causing elevated suction pressure and reduced cooling efficiency. It's crucial to refer to manufacturer specifications to ensure the correct piston size is used. If uncertain, replace the piston with the recommended size, then re-evaluate system performance.

Subcooling Analysis

Subcooling, the process where liquid refrigerant is cooled below its condensation point, is vital in assessing piston systems. Unlike TXV systems, where subcooling values remain relatively stable, subcooling in piston systems can fluctuate based on load conditions. The typical subcooling range for piston systems varies between 5° to 23°, with an average observation around 10° +/- 3° during normal operations (Source: Orr, 2020).

Guideline: To interpret subcooling accurately, measure the temperature difference between the liquid line leaving the condenser and the liquid saturation temperature corresponding to the condenser's outlet pressure. High subcooling may indicate overcharging or a restriction in the liquid line, while low subcooling suggests undercharging or excessive refrigerant flow past the piston. Consistently monitor subcooling readings to diagnose and correct potential issues swiftly.

Common Problems Indicated by Gauge Readings

Piston systems can reveal a myriad of operational issues through their gauge readings, allowing technicians to troubleshoot effectively.

1. **Low Suction Pressure** : Often indicates problems like low refrigerant charge, reduced airflow due to dirty filters or evaporators, or restrictions within the metering device. For

instance, a clogged piston or an incorrectly sized one will manifest as low suction pressure.

1. **High Suction Pressure** : Typically results from overcharging, where too much refrigerant is present within the system. It might also suggest high ambient temperatures affecting the condensing unit or an inefficient compressor not achieving the necessary compression ratio.

1. **Low Subcooling** : Suggests that the system is undercharged or experiencing issues like a metering device allowing too much refrigerant flow due to a large piston or improperly seated piston. Additional reasons include compressor inefficiencies where it fails to pump adequately, causing low refrigerant pressure.

1. **High Subcooling** : Indicates overcharging, or a restricted metering device often due to a small piston size. Other causes could be blockages within the liquid line, dirty condenser coils raising the condensing temperature, or even a heat reclaim unit installed, which isn't common but possible.

1. **High Evaporator Air Temperature Split (Delta T)** : A narrow temperature difference across the evaporator coil points to issues such as low airflow—often tied to obstructions like dirty air filters—or blower malfunctions. In some cases, it

might indicate an unusually low humidity level impacting the air temperature split.

1. **Low Evaporator Air Temperature Split** : On the other hand, a wide temperature difference might signal undercharging, severe overcharging with a fixed orifice, inadequate functioning of the metering device, or excessive airflow through the evaporator. Be vigilant about other contributing factors like abnormally high humidity levels, compressor inefficiencies, or bypassing reversing valves.

Core Message

Understanding the differences in gauge readings between TXV and piston systems is essential for effective HVAC diagnostics. This chapter has detailed the specific indicators that technicians should look for when evaluating system performance. In TXV systems, we discussed how pressure differentials and the temperature-pressure relationship reveal the system's operational status, while superheat calculations help ensure optimal refrigerant flow. Recognizing common symptoms like fluctuating pressures and unusual superheat values allows technicians to diagnose and address potential problems promptly.

In contrast, piston systems require a different approach due to their fixed refrigerant flow characteristics. The chapter outlined how static pressure measurements, subcooling analysis, and common gauge reading issues can highlight problems such as improper piston sizing, refrigerant overcharge, or restrictions in the liquid line. By comparing these diagnostic techniques, HVAC professionals can gain a comprehensive understanding of how to leverage digital gauges to accurately identify whether an HVAC system uses a TXV or a piston. This knowledge is crucial for making informed decisions during troubleshooting and ensuring optimal system performance.

Reference List

Orr, B. (2020, February 17). *The Five Pillars Of Residential A/C Refrigerant Circuit Diagnosis* . Achrnews.com; ACHR News. https://www.achrnews.com/articles/142656-the-five-pillarsof-residential-ac-refrigerant-circuit-diagnosis

Orr, B. (2020, July 27). *What Should My Superheat Be? - HVAC School* . HVAC School. https://hvacrschool.com/what-should-my-superheat-be/

Orr, B. (2019, July 24). *The "5 Pillars" of Residential A/C Refrigerant Circuit Diagnosis - HVAC School* . HVAC School. https://hvacrschool.com/the-5-pillarsof-residential-ac-refrigerant-circuit-diagnosis/

Tomczyk, J. (2018, July 2). *Seven Signs of Low Refrigerant in a System* . Achrnews.com; ACHR News. https://www.achrnews.com/articles/137329seven-signs-of-low-refrigerant-in-a-system

chapter 4

Capacitor Testing Basics

Testing capacitors is a fundamental skill for any HVAC technician, requiring precision and attention to detail. This chapter will guide you through the essential steps of using a voltmeter to measure microfarads (MFD) with the HVAC unit turned off. This approach not only ensures that you obtain accurate readings but also prioritizes safety, which is paramount in any electrical work.

In this chapter, you will learn about the tools needed for testing capacitors, including a reliable digital voltmeter and appropriate test leads, as well as the importance of discharging the capacitor safely using a resistor. We will cover the step-by-step process of disconnecting the capacitor from its circuit and ensuring it's free of residual voltage. Techniques for accurately measuring MFD and common mistakes to avoid will be discussed in detail. By the end of this chapter, you will be equipped with the knowledge and skills to test capacitors confidently and effectively, ensuring the proper functioning of HVAC systems.

Using a Voltmeter to Measure MFD

Using a voltmeter to measure microfarads (MFD) plays a decisive role in assessing the functionality of capacitors, especially within HVAC systems. Understanding this process not only sharpens a technician's skills but also ensures safety and precision in diagnosing capacitor-related issues.

Essential tools for measuring capacitors involve having a reliable digital voltmeter and appropriate test leads. A digital multimeter capable of measuring capacitance is essential for providing accurate readings. The test leads, which connect the multimeter to the capacitor terminals, must be in good condition to avoid false readings or potential hazards. Additionally, having a resistor to safely discharge the capacitor is crucial.

The process of properly disconnecting a capacitor from its circuit involves several careful steps. First, ensure all power to the HVAC unit is turned off. Use the multimeter to confirm there is no residual voltage by checking both AC and DC settings depending on the circuit type. Wearing personal protective equipment, such as insulated gloves, prevents accidental contact with energized components. Next, discharge the capacitor using a 20,000 Ω, 5-watt resistor. Attach this resistor across the capacitor terminals for at least five seconds. Finally, visually inspect the capacitor's physical condition. Look for any signs of leaks, bulges, cracks, or other damages which signal that the capacitor needs replacement before proceeding with testing.

To measure MFD accurately, start by setting the multimeter to the capacitance measurement mode. This symbolic setting often shares a dial position with another function, so refer to the user manual if needed. With the capacitor removed from the circuit, connect the test leads to the capacitor terminals. Hold the leads in place for a few moments to allow the multimeter to stabilize and select the proper range automatically. Read the displayed value, which should fall within the range marked on the capacitor. If the multimeter shows 'OL' (overload), it means the capacitor's value is higher than the device's measured range or the capacitor may be faulty.

Common mistakes can occur during the measurement process if care isn't taken. One frequent error is failing to verify that the circuit power is completely off, leading to potentially dangerous situations. Another mistake is not fully discharging the capacitor, which can give inaccurate readings and pose an electric shock hazard. Additionally, connecting the leads incorrectly or not securing them firmly enough can result in poor contact and unreliable measurements. Using worn-out test leads can also affect accuracy, so it's vital to regularly inspect and replace them if necessary.

When testing capacitors, keep in mind these critical points to achieve precise measurements. Always work in a methodical manner, double-checking each step to ensure safety and accuracy. Proper technique not only enhances the reliability of your readings but also extends the lifespan of your tools and the components you're working with. By avoiding common pitfalls and adhering to correct procedures, technicians can confidently diagnose and resolve issues related to capacitors in HVAC systems.

Interpreting Capacitor Test Results

Understanding manufacturer specifications is crucial when analyzing capacitor test results. Every capacitor comes labeled with an MFD (microfarads) rating, which indicates its capacitance value. This rating can be found on the capacitor's body and represents the capacitor's ability to store charge. Reading these labels accurately is essential as they provide a benchmark for comparison during testing.

Identifying acceptable ranges for readings involves knowing the tolerances specified by the manufacturer. Capacitors are designed to operate within certain limits, and their actual measured capacitance can vary slightly from the stated value. For instance, a capacitor marked 40 MFD might have an acceptable range of 38 MFD to 42 MFD. Understanding these tolerances helps technicians determine if a capacitor is functioning properly or needs replacement.

Comparing actual readings to manufacturer's specifications enhances diagnosis accuracy. By ensuring the measured capacitance falls within the manufacturer's specified range, technicians can confidently assess whether a capacitor is working correctly. If the readings are outside the acceptable range, this indicates a potential issue with the capacitor, necessitating further investigation or replacement.

Correlating test results with performance issues is another important skill. HVAC systems rely heavily on capacitors, and any deviations in capacitance can affect system performance. For example, a lowerthan-expected capacitance reading could result in a compressor not starting or running inefficiently. Technicians should be able to connect these test results to specific performance problems within the

HVAC system, allowing them to target repairs more effectively.

Real-life scenarios help illustrate the importance of interpreting data correctly. Consider a scenario where an HVAC unit repeatedly fails to start. Testing reveals that the run capacitor's measured capacitance is significantly below its rating. Recognizing this discrepancy allows the technician to replace the faulty capacitor, restoring the unit's functionality. Understanding how to interpret test results in context is key to effective troubleshooting.

The importance of tolerances in readings enables technicians to distinguish between functional and faulty components. A slight deviation within the tolerance range might not immediately indicate a problem. However, repeated patterns of degradation over time, such as continually decreasing capacitance values, could signal upcoming failures. Knowing how to interpret these trends helps in making informed maintenance decisions.

Training technicians to think critically encourages proactive problem-solving skills. By understanding how capacitor performance impacts overall HVAC functionality, technicians can anticipate issues before they escalate. Critical thinking also promotes continuous learning and adaptation to new technologies or specifications that might arise in the field.

Documenting test results for future reference is a best practice that should not be overlooked. Recording MFD measurements, along with the date and any relevant observations, creates a valuable log for tracking the health of capacitors over time. These records can be referenced during future maintenance checks or when diagnosing intermittent issues, providing a clear history of past performance.

Promoting documentation emphasizes the importance of tracking maintenance history. This practice ensures consistency in monitoring equipment health and supports better decisionmaking processes. When an HVAC system is serviced, having detailed records of past capacitor tests can pinpoint recurring issues or confirm the effectiveness of previous repairs.

Recording results fosters continuous learning and improvement within the technician's practice. Reviewing past records enables technicians to identify patterns and refine their diagnostic approaches. This habit not only improves individual skill sets but also contributes to the broader knowledge base within a team or organization.

Clear notes facilitate diagnostics during repeat service calls, enhancing customer trust. When a technician returns to a job site, having access to previous test results speeds up the troubleshooting process. It demonstrates professionalism and thoroughness to clients, building confidence in the technician's abilities and fostering long-term client relationships.

Final Thoughts

In this chapter, we delved into the essential methods and tools required to test capacitors within HVAC systems using a voltmeter. Emphasizing safety and accuracy, we covered the step-by-step procedure of safely disconnecting, discharging, and measuring the capacitor's microfarad (MFD) value. By understanding and implementing these techniques, technicians can confidently diagnose capacitor issues without risking their own safety or that of the equipment.

We also explored how to interpret the test results by comparing them to manufacturer specifications and tolerances. Recognizing acceptable ranges and correlating measured capacitance with HVAC performance issues are crucial skills for technicians. Proper documentation of test results supports ongoing maintenance and helps identify patterns of degradation over time. This proactive approach not only enhances diagnostic accuracy but also fosters continuous learning and improves overall system reliability.

Reference List

(2021). Repairfaq.org. https://www.repairfaq.org/sam/captest.htm

Ceramic Capacitor FAQ and Application Guide . (n.d.). Www.kemet.com. https://www.kemet.com/en/us/capacitors/ceramic/ceramics-faq.html

Fluke. (2020, October 15). *How to Measure Capacitance with a Digital Multimeter* . Fluke.com. https://www.fluke.com/en-us/learn/blog/digitalmultimeters/how-to-measure-capacitance?srsltid=AfmBOopEDeOgKjFo54KWoIUFyqNtUd61XvQb53I33nmLNZVNCBHtiSY

Joy, A. T. (n.d.). *How to Test a Capacitor With a Multimeter* . Tameson.com. https://tameson.com/pages/capacitor-multimeter

chapter 5

Live Capacitor Testing

Testing capacitors in live units involves specific techniques and precautions to ensure both safety and accuracy. Live capacitor testing requires the use of appropriate tools and methods to measure and diagnose without de-energizing the unit. By focusing on real-time diagnostics, technicians can gain insights into a capacitor's performance under actual operating conditions, which is vital for effective troubleshooting and maintenance. This process stresses the importance of precision and care when handling live electrical components, as it combines technical skills with rigorous safety protocols.

This chapter will guide you through the comprehensive procedures for live capacitor testing, emphasizing the role of a voltmeter in ensuring reliable measurements. It will detail essential safety measures, such as wearing Personal Protective Equipment (PPE) and following best practices to mitigate risks associated with high-voltage environments. You will also learn about the importance of systematic approaches and the use of circuit verification tools to confirm the absence of electrical currents before proceeding. Additionally, the chapter will cover calculating the microfarad (MFD) rating using amp readings, a crucial skill for maintaining system efficiency and performance. Each step, from preparation to execution, will be outlined to enhance your understanding and confidence in performing live capacitor tests safely and accurately.

Safety Precautions for Live Testing

When testing capacitors in live units, technicians must observe essential safety measures to avoid hazards and ensure proper procedures.

Understanding electrical hazards is paramount. Capacitors in HVAC systems can carry high voltages, which pose significant risks such as severe injuries or even fatalities. Technicians should be aware of these operational characteristics and maintain clarity in their workspace. High voltage can cause electric shocks, burns, and other life-threatening conditions. Therefore, recognizing the potential dangers and maintaining a clean and organized work environment is critical.

The use of Personal Protective Equipment (PPE) can't be overstated. PPE forms the first line of defense against electrical hazards. Technicians should always wear gear like insulated gloves, goggles, and insulation mats when handling live capacitors. Insulated gloves protect against electric shocks, while goggles shield the eyes from potential sparks or debris. Insulation mats provide a non-conductive surface, reducing the risk of electrical grounding through the technician's body. Compliant equipment types, such as those meeting NFPA 70E standards, should be used to ensure maximum safety. For instance, dielectric boots can further insulate the technician and prevent electricity from passing through their body if they accidentally come into contact with live conductors.

Adhering to safety protocols and emergency procedures is another crucial aspect. Best practices include using tools that are rated for the specific environment and regular inspections of these tools for any signs of damage or wear. Emergency tools, such as fire extinguishers and first aid kits, should always be readily accessible. Additionally, having communication devices on hand ensures that help can be summoned quickly in case of an accident. Shutdown procedures must be clearly understood and followed diligently to safely de-energize circuits before working on them whenever possible. In cases where live testing is necessary, these procedures become even more critical. Adherence to established safety protocols prevents mishaps and ensures that every step taken minimizes risks.

Isolation techniques and circuit verification are vital methods for ensuring safety during live capacitor tests. Methods for circuit isolation assurance involve using lockout/tagout procedures to prevent accidental re-energizing. This method ensures that no one else can turn on the circuit while maintenance or inspection is underway. Visual inspections should be conducted meticulously to identify any loose connections, damaged wires, or other potential hazards. Circuit tracer tools can be employed to verify the de-energized state of circuits before beginning work. These tools help confirm that there is no electrical current present, providing an added layer of assurance. Promoting caution and thoroughness in these processes helps prevent inadvertent exposure to live electrical parts.

Technicians should follow a systematic approach to these safety measures, ensuring all checks and preparations are completed before starting any live testing. Understanding the specifics of how each piece of PPE functions can make a significant difference in its effective use. For example, knowing that certain insulation gloves have specific voltage ratings can help technicians select the appropriate pair for a particular job. Detailed knowledge about the correct use of circuit verification tools, such as how to properly ground a probe to get an accurate reading, is equally important.

Moreover, continuous education and training play a significant role in maintaining safety standards. Regular training sessions on the latest safety protocols, emergency procedures, and the correct use of PPE keep technicians informed and prepared. It's also beneficial to conduct mock emergency drills to ensure that everyone knows what to do in case of an actual incident. Such proactive measures foster a culture of safety and readiness among technicians.

Calculating MFD with Amps Formula

Calculating the microfarad (MFD) rating of a capacitor using amp readings from a live unit is an essential skill for HVAC technicians. This practical application of electrical principles is crucial for troubleshooting and maintaining system performance.

First, let's understand the relationship between amperage and microfarads. The formula for calculating MFD from amperage readings is based on electrical theory. Specifically, you use the start winding amps, multiply by the constant 2,652, and then divide by the capacitor voltage. The formula can be written as:

$$ \text{Microfarads} = \frac{\text{Start Winding Amps} \times 2652}{\text{Capacitor Voltage}} $$

This relationship is vital because it allows technicians to assess whether a capacitor is functioning correctly while the unit is operating under load conditions. A correctly functioning capacitor ensures that the motor receives proper phase shift and increased starting torque needed for efficient operation. Poor performance or failure in capacitors can lead to inefficient systems, higher operational costs, and potential system damage.

Now, let's delve into the step-by-step calculation process. This guideline will help ensure accuracy in your MFD calculations. Consistent measurement and meticulous attention to detail are key.

1. **Gather Initial Readings** : Turn on the HVAC unit and allow it to operate for about 5-10 minutes to stabilize. This period helps achieve accurate readings under typical operating conditions.

1. **Measure Amperage** : Use a clamp meter to measure the amperage of the start wire. This wire connects the capacitor to the compressor. For most motors, this will be the brown wire without a white stripe. Note the amperage reading.

1. **Measure Voltage** : With a voltmeter, measure the voltage across the capacitor terminals. For a compressor, this would involve measuring between

the Herm (HERM) and Common (C) terminals, while for a condenser fan motor, measure between the Fan (FAN) and Common (C) terminals. Record the voltage reading.

1. **Apply the Formula** : Multiply the amperage reading by 2,652, then divide the result by the voltage reading. This calculation gives the MFD value of the capacitor.

For instance, if the amperage reading on the start wire is 4.4 amps and the voltage across the capacitor is 297 volts, the calculation would be as follows:

$$ \text{MFD} = \frac{4.4 \times 2652}{297} = 39.3 $$

1. **Compare with Nameplate Rating** : Compare the calculated MFD with the capacitor's nameplate rating. Most capacitors have a tolerance range, typically +/- 6%. If your calculated value falls outside this range, the capacitor may need replacing. For example, if the nameplate rating is 40 MFD, acceptable values lie between 37.6 and 42.4 MFD.

1. **Repeat for All Run Capacitors** : Perform the same procedure for all run capacitors in the system to ensure each is functioning correctly under load.

It's important to illustrate these steps with real-life examples. Consider an HVAC technician who identifies a cooling issue in a residential air conditioning unit. Upon testing the start wire amperage at 6.1 amps and measuring the voltage at 297 volts, the calculation reveals the MFD as follows:

$$ \text{MFD} = \frac{6.1 \times 2652}{297} = 54.5 $$

If the capacitor's nameplate rating is 45 MFD, and given the 6% tolerance range (42.3 to 47.7 MFD), the

54.5 MFD is significantly outside this range, indicating the capacitor should be replaced.

Connecting these findings to system performance highlights the importance of accurate MFD calculations. When calculated values indicate deviations from the expected range, it signals the need for maintenance or replacement. Replacing weak or faulty capacitors ensures motors operate efficiently, reducing wear and tear and preventing potential breakdowns. Over time, this practice enhances the reliability and lifespan of HVAC systems, ensuring consistent performance and energy efficiency.

Final Insights

Safety and accuracy are paramount when testing capacitors in live units. This chapter detailed critical safety measures, emphasizing the importance of understanding electrical hazards and using appropriate Personal Protective Equipment (PPE). Techniques such as isolation methods and circuit verification were underscored to prevent accidental exposure to live electrical parts. By adhering to established safety protocols and maintaining regular training, technicians can ensure a safer working environment and be better prepared for any emergencies.

Additionally, the chapter provided a step-by-step guide for calculating the microfarad (MFD) rating of a capacitor using amperage readings. Understanding this calculation is essential for diagnosing and maintaining HVAC systems effectively. Regular comparison between calculated MFD values and nameplate ratings helps identify faulty capacitors, ensuring optimal system performance and longevity. Through meticulous application of these procedures, HVAC technicians can enhance their diagnostic capabilities and contribute to more efficient and reliable system operations.

Reference List

Electrical Safety in Electronics Manufacturing . (2021, March 22). https://www.lectronixinc.com/ electrical-safety-in-electronics-manufacturing/

How to check a capacitor while the system is running. – Carrier Enterprise Mid-Atlantic Technical Support Site . (2019). Cematraining.com. https://cematraining.com/how-to-check-a-capacitorwhile-the-system-is-running/

Orr, B. (2017, March 4). *Testing Run Capacitors the Smart (and Easy) Way - HVAC School* . HVAC School. https://hvacrschool.com/testing-runcapacitors-smart-easy-way/

Smith, B. D., & Nov 01, 2006. (n.d.). *Safety Considerations for Live Electrical Measurements - .* Occupational Health & Safety. https:// ohsonline.com/Articles/2006/11/SafetyConsiderations-for-Live-ElectricalMeasurements.aspx

chapter 6

Wiring Universal Condenser Fan Motors

Wiring 110-volt universal condenser fan motors requires a clear understanding of the necessary steps to ensure accuracy and dependability. This process is fundamental for HVAC technicians who need to establish reliable connections to maintain optimal motor performance. By approaching each step methodically, the risk of errors decreases, resulting in successful installations and troubleshooting.

This chapter will guide you through the essential components of wiring diagrams and their interpretation, focusing on power supply lines, motors, capacitors, and other crucial elements. You'll learn how to read diagrams step-by-step, understand color coding in wiring, and apply this knowledge practically. By the end of the chapter, you'll be equipped with the skills to connect motors to contactors, test the connections thoroughly, and troubleshoot any issues that may arise, ensuring each installation functions smoothly and efficiently.

Dutch Pearson

Basic Wiring Diagram Explanation

Understanding the components in a wiring diagram is essential for anyone working with universal condenser fan motors. To begin, let's delve into the standard components usually depicted in these diagrams.

Typically, a wiring diagram for a condenser fan motor will include the power supply lines, the motor itself, and a capacitor. The power supply lines are often labeled L1 and L2 or T1 and T2, representing the main electrical connections. The motor, an essential component, will be shown with various wires extending from it, each designated to carry out specific functions. Capacitors are also crucial as they help start the motor and improve its efficiency. In addition, you might notice symbols for ground connections and switches.

Given this foundation, understanding these components ensures that technicians can identify each part's role within the larger system. Recognizing these elements helps avoid common mistakes during installation and maintenance.

Reading a wiring diagram step-by-step is necessary to grasp how each component connects and interacts within the system. Start by locating the power source on the diagram. This is usually illustrated at the top or bottom of the page and may be labeled with notations like L1 and L2 or T1 and T2, indicating line voltage terminals connected to the power supply.

Next, trace the path from the power source to the condenser fan motor. Follow each wire as it leads to different components such as capacitors and contactors. Pay attention to any intersecting lines, which indicate points where wires connect. Special notations like dots or junctions signify these intersections.

Wires are often represented by specific colors: white for neutral, black for live, and green or bare for ground. Identifying these colors helps formulate a clear picture of the circuit. Diagrams may also include labels like "Fan," "Compressor," or "Capacitor," providing additional context on each wire's destination.

When interpreting a wiring diagram, focus on the sequence of the connections. For instance, observe if the white wire from the condenser fan motor connects to one side of the power on the contactor (T1) and jumps to one side of the fan capacitor. Carefully follow how the black wire connects to the other side of the power on the contactor (T2) and how the brown wire connects to the other side of the capacitor opposite the jumper wire. This step-by-step process clarifies the relationship between different components and their collective operation.

Color coding in wiring diagrams plays a significant role in ensuring safe and efficient installations. Wire colors offer visual cues that simplify identifying electrical pathways and prevent errors. Standard color codes are widely used in HVAC systems, where specific colors correspond to certain functions. For example, brown wires typically connect to capacitors, white wires indicate neutral connections, and black wires represent live connections.

Although wire colors can vary between manufacturers, adherence to standard color codes in service replacement motors provides consistency, reducing the potential for confusion. It's important to remember that while the colors tend to be consistent, they technically hold no intrinsic meaning. Always refer to the specific wiring diagram for the motor being used to confirm connections.

In practical application, understanding wiring diagrams empowers technicians to tackle real-world scenarios effectively. For example, when tasked with replacing a 3-wire motor with a 4-wire model, a thorough comprehension of the diagram simplifies the process. A technician would note that a 3-wire setup involves connecting the white wire from the fan motor to one side of the power on the contactor (T1), jumping to one side of the fan capacitor, connecting the black wire to the other side of the power on the contactor (T2), and attaching the brown wire to the other side of the capacitor.

Switching to a 4-wire configuration, they would identify that the white wire now connects to one side of power on the contactor (T1). The black wire attaches to the other side of power on the contactor (T2). The brown wire goes to the capacitor, similar to the 3-wire setup, but there's an additional brown + white wire that also connects to the capacitor.

Real-world application extends beyond simple replacements. Suppose a technician's task is to diagnose a malfunctioning condenser fan motor. They could use the wiring diagram to systematically check each connection point. By following the diagram, they can verify that each wire is correctly positioned and determine whether any components like capacitors have failed.

Moreover, diagrams can aid in troubleshooting more complex issues. For example, if a new motor isn't starting, the technician can use the wiring diagram to ensure all connections are correct. If problems persist, examining the continuity of wires with an ohmmeter against the diagram can reveal breaks or faults in the circuitry.

Overall, breaking down a typical wiring diagram provides readers with the knowledge needed to visualize and understand the necessary connections for universal condenser fan motors. By comprehending the components, reading the diagram step-by-step, recognizing the importance of color coding, and applying this knowledge practically, technicians can perform accurate and reliable installations and maintenance.

Sources:

Orr, 2019

Connecting Motors to the Contactor

When wiring 110-volt universal condenser fan motors, the process of connecting these motors to a contactor is critical. By following accurate steps and understanding key components, technicians can ensure each installation's reliability and functionality without risking damage or failure.

Identifying Terminals on the Contactor

Understanding the layout of terminals on a contactor is fundamental. Generally, contactors have three types of terminals: the coil terminals, load terminals, and auxiliary terminals. Coil terminals connect to a low-voltage circuit that triggers the switch inside the contactor. Load terminals carry the high current needed for the motor's operation. Auxiliary terminals often control additional features like indicator lights or safety devices.

For example, in a typical setup, the coil terminals might be labeled A1 and A2, with terminal A1 connected to a control signal and terminal A2 grounded. The load terminals, usually labeled L1, L2, and L3, are where the main power lines connect. By correctly identifying these terminals, technicians prevent miswiring, which can lead to equipment malfunction or hazards.

Wiring Procedure

To wire the motor correctly:

1. **Safety First** : Ensure all power sources are turned off and locked out to prevent accidental energization.

2. **Prepare the Wires** : Strip the insulation off the ends of the wires to expose enough conductor material for a secure connection.

3. **Connect the Coil Terminals** : Attach one end of the control circuit wire to terminal A1 and the other end to the appropriate control device, then ground terminal A2.

4. **Attach the Load Terminals** : Connect the power supply wires to the load terminals L1, L2, and L3. These should align with the corresponding phase lines from the power source.

5. **Verify Tight Connections** : Ensure all terminal screws are tightened securely to avoid loose connections, which can cause arcing or overheating.

6. **Connect the Motor Leads** : Finally, connect the motor leads to the output side of the load terminals, adhering to any specific color coding or local electrical codes.

Following these steps helps in establishing a solid and reliable connection between the motor and the contactor, ensuring the motor receives the necessary power for operation.

Testing Connections

Testing connections after wiring is crucial to confirm proper installation:

1. **Visual Inspection** : Check all wires for correct placement and tightness. Look for signs of wear or damage on wires that could lead to faults.

2. **Continuity Test** : Using a digital multimeter, perform a continuity test to verify there are no breaks in the circuit. This ensures that electrical paths are complete and capable of conducting electricity.

3. **Voltage Test** : Once the system is powered on, measure the voltage at various points to ensure it matches expected values. Incorrect voltage levels can indicate miswiring or faulty components.

4. **Functional Test** : Activate the control circuit to engage the contactor. Listen for a clicking sound that indicates the contactor is functioning properly. Observe the motor to see if it starts and runs smoothly without unusual noise or vibration.

These tests provide confidence that the connection is sound and the system will operate as intended.

Troubleshooting Connection Issues

Despite careful wiring, issues can still arise. Common problems include:

1. **Contactor Fails to Engage** : This could result from insufficient control voltage, a burned-out coil, or a mechanical jam within the contactor. Verify the control voltage meets specifications and test the coil resistance using a multimeter. If the coil shows an open circuit, it must be replaced.

2. **Motor Does Not Start** : This might happen due to incorrect wiring, poor connections, or a faulty motor. Double-check the wiring against the schematic, retighten all connections, and ensure the motor is functional by testing it separately.

3. **Intermittent Operation** : This can occur because of low control voltage, worn contacts, or overloaded circuits. Measure the control voltage to ensure it remains steady and inspect contact surfaces for pitting or burning. An overloaded

circuit may require redistributing the load or upgrading the circuit capacity.

4. **Overheating Components** : Overheating is often due to loose connections or excessive current flow. Make sure all connections are snug and use a clamp meter to measure current draw, comparing it against the motor's rated current.

In cases of complex or persistent problems, consulting a qualified electrician is advisable to diagnose and resolve the issue accurately.

Closing Remarks

In this chapter, we have laid out the essential steps for wiring 110-volt universal condenser fan motors. Emphasis was placed on understanding the wiring diagram components, identifying correct terminal connections on the contactor, and following a systematic wiring procedure. These steps are critical in ensuring that technicians can achieve reliable and safe motor operation. By mastering these elements, technicians can avoid common mistakes and ensure each installation's success.

Additionally, we explored methods for testing connections to confirm proper installation and covered potential troubleshooting scenarios. Testing includes visual inspections, continuity tests, voltage measurements, and functional assessments, all of which are vital for identifying and resolving issues. Troubleshooting tips were provided to address frequent problems such as contactor failures, motor start issues, intermittent operation, and overheating. Armed with this knowledge, technicians are better equipped to handle real-world challenges and ensure effective and efficient motor wiring.

Reference List

Contactor Testing: A Beginner's Guide to Safety & Basics . (2024, July 12). Geya.net. http://www.geya.net/contactor-testing-guide/

DoItYourself.com Community Forums. (n.d.). *Universal blower motor wire colors - Help!!* Retrieved from https://www.doityourself.com/ forum/heat-pumps-electric-home-heating/640545universal-blower-motor-wire-colors-help.html

Johnson, N. (2023, February 16). *How do I Test Relays and Contactors?* Maintenance World. https://

maintenanceworld.com/2023/02/16/how-do-i-testrelays-and-contactors/

Orr, B. (2019, August 21). *3-Wire and 4-Wire Condensing Fan Motor Connection - HVAC School* . HVAC School. https://hvacrschool.com/3-wire-4wire-condensing-fan-motor-connection/

chapter 7

Installing Universal Blower Motors

Installing universal blower motors in indoor HVAC units requires a careful and systematic approach. This chapter explains the process to ensure that each motor functions efficiently and safely within various HVAC setups. Attention to wiring details is critical, as improper connections can lead to significant operational issues or even hazardous situations. The content is crafted to guide technicians through the essential steps needed to complete these installations confidently, using clear instructions and reliable visual aids.

This chapter will dive into creating detailed wiring diagrams that outline specific color codes and terminal designations for universal blower motors. Technicians will learn how to recognize and secure key connections, such as power supply, ground, and control signals, which are vital for proper motor operation. Additionally, this section covers common wiring scenarios and techniques for adapting them to different unit setups, ensuring compatibility across various systems. Verification methods for checking all connections before powering up the motor will also be discussed, highlighting the importance of meticulousness to prevent installation mistakes and system failures.

Simple Wiring Diagram for Blower Motors

When wiring universal blower motors for indoor HVAC units, it is crucial to follow a systematic approach to ensure successful installation and operation. This subpoint aims to clarify the wiring process for universal blower motors by providing readers with reliable visual aids and specific instructions that empower them to complete installations confidently and avoid potential mistakes.

Creating a clear wiring diagram is essential for outlining specific color codes and terminal designations necessary for proper wiring. Typically, universal blower motors come with various wires, each designated for different functions such as highspeed, medium-speed, low-speed, power supply, ground, and control signals. Documenting these connections in a clean, straightforward wiring diagram helps technicians visualize the setup and reduces the likelihood of errors during the installation process.

A sample wiring diagram might indicate that black represents high speed, blue is for medium speed, red signifies low speed, white denotes the common wire or neutral, and green symbolizes the ground. By clearly labeling these wires and their respective terminals on the motor and corresponding placements in the HVAC unit, technicians can reference the diagram to perform accurate and efficient installations.

Identifying key connections is another critical aspect of the wiring process. Key connections generally include the power supply, ground, and control signals. For instance, ensuring that the motor's power supply wires are correctly connected to the appropriate terminals prevents electrical problems and allows the motor to function effectively. Identifying the ground connection is equally important, as connecting it properly ensures safety by preventing potential short circuits or electrical shocks. Finally, control signals— often represented by wires connected to the thermostat or control board— must be accurately linked to manage the motor's speed and operational status.

To prevent installation mistakes and system failures, it's vital to explore various common wiring scenarios encountered in different unit setups. Universal blower motors are designed to fit multiple HVAC systems, so compatibility issues must be addressed. For example, some units may require a three-wire connection, while others need four wires.

Understanding these distinctions and adapting to the specific needs of each setup will better prepare technicians for real-world challenges. When an HVAC unit operates under unique conditions (e.g., singlephase vs. three-phase power), acknowledging these variations and adjusting the wiring accordingly is necessary for a successful installation.

Verifying all connections after wiring is a step that cannot be overlooked. Before powering up the motor, double-check every connection to make sure they are secure and correctly placed. Incorrect wiring can lead to severe consequences, including motor failure, damage to the HVAC system, or even electrical fires. One practical method of verification is to use a multimeter to test the continuity and voltage at each connection point, confirming that electricity flows appropriately without any shorts. This precaution helps identify and rectify mistakes before they cause significant issues.

For instance, when faced with a situation where the motor does not run in "Heat" mode with the Fan set to "Auto," as discussed in the DoItYourself.com Community Forums, this typically indicates a wiring issue related to control signals. Rechecking the connections against a clear wiring diagram and verifying each wire's placement using a multimeter can resolve such problems (DoItYourself.com Community Forums, n.d.).

In conclusion, understanding and implementing a structured wiring process is paramount for installing universal blower motors successfully. By creating clear wiring diagrams, identifying and securing key connections, exploring common wiring scenarios, and meticulously verifying all connections, technicians can ensure safe, efficient, and reliable installations.

References:

Ensuring Proper Motor Configuration

Correctly configuring the blower motor is crucial for achieving optimal performance and supporting efficient HVAC operation. This process begins with understanding motor ratings, including horsepower (HP) and speed settings. Motor ratings are vital indicators that help technicians choose the most appropriate motor for a given application. For instance, selecting a motor with the correct horsepower ensures it can handle the necessary workload without overstressing, which might lead to premature failure.

Typically, a higher HP motor is needed for larger systems requiring significant airflow to maintain adequate temperature control. Alongside horsepower, the motor's speed settings, often measured in revolutions per minute (RPM), play a critical role. The ability to select the right RPM setting is fundamental since the speed at which the motor operates directly influences the airflow rate and, consequently, the efficiency of the entire system.

Configuring the speed settings of the blower motor based on system requirements and user preferences significantly impacts the comfort levels within the indoor environment. Variable-speed motors, such as ECMs (Electronically Commutated Motors), offer exceptional flexibility by enabling precise adjustments to meet varying demands. These motors can adapt their speed to match the changing needs of the HVAC system, ensuring constant and efficient airflow. Guidelines for configuring these speed settings include assessing the specific cooling or heating load of the space and determining the desired comfort level, whether it's improved airflow during peak summer heat or maintaining warmer air circulation during colder months. Following these guidelines ensures the system runs optimally, reducing energy consumption and enhancing overall indoor comfort.

Proper mounting and alignment of the blower motor are essential to minimize vibrations and mechanical wear issues. Improper installation can lead to several problems, including increased noise levels, reduced efficiency, and accelerated wear and tear of the motor and associated components. To ensure proper mounting, technicians should securely fasten the motor to avoid any movement during operation. Aligning the motor accurately with the blower wheel or fan is equally important; misalignment can cause imbalanced rotation, resulting in excessive vibrations. Using a laser alignment tool can be particularly effective for achieving precision. Addressing these aspects not only prolongs the motor's lifespan but also helps in maintaining a quieter and more efficient HVAC system.

Conducting tests following installation is a critical step to ensure the motor operates as intended. Once the motor is installed and configured, technicians must perform a series of tests to verify its performance. This includes checking the electrical connections to ensure they are secure and within the specified voltage and amperage ranges. Running the motor at different speeds allows technicians to observe its operation under various conditions and identify any issues early on. For example, a common test involves measuring the airflow and checking it against the expected values for the particular system configuration. Any discrepancies might indicate the need for further adjustments or potential issues that need addressing before they escalate into major problems. Additionally, monitoring the motor's temperature during operation can reveal if it's overheating, which could be a sign of excessive friction or incorrect wiring.

Summary and Reflections

This chapter has delved into essential guidelines for wiring and installing universal blower motors in indoor HVAC units, aiming to equip technicians with the knowledge needed for effective and safe execution. We've emphasized the importance of clear wiring diagrams, color-coded wire identification, and the securing of key connections such as power supply and ground. Technicians must understand various wiring scenarios they might encounter, including three-wire and four-wire setups, and adapt accordingly to ensure compatibility with different HVAC systems.

Additionally, we addressed the critical steps of verifying all connections before powering up the motor and using tools like multimeters for accuracy. Proper motor configuration, including understanding horsepower, speed settings, and ensuring precise alignment, is vital for optimal performance and system efficiency. Conducting post-installation tests further ensures that the motor operates correctly under various conditions. By following these comprehensive guidelines, technicians can enhance the reliability and longevity of HVAC units, ensuring a safer and more comfortable indoor environment.

Reference List

DoItYourself.com Community Forums. (n.d.). *Universal blower motor wire colors - Help!!* . Retrieved from https://www.doityourself.com/forum/heat-pumps-electric-home-heating/640545universal-blower-motor-wire-colors-help.html

Eck, L. (2023, July 21). *A Deep Dive into AC Blower Motors* . Liberty Supply; Liberty Supply. https://libertysupply.com/blogs/hvac-news/ac-blowermotor?srsltid=AfmBOoriEsIqUPuCZLKsndWRLlfyvcHisnQ2KpOVHKMp5EAx6quGzuOR

Migliacco, C. (2021, May 19). *Adjusting the Airflow Speed on ECM Blower Fan Motors! (Variable & Multi-*

Speed Types) . AC Service Tech, LLC. https://www.acservicetech.com/post/adjusting-airflowspeed-on-an-ecm-blower-motor

for, W. (2015, October 31). *Correct Wiring for Furnace Blower Motor* . Home Improvement Stack Exchange. https://diy.stackexchange.com/questions/77130/correct-wiring-for-furnace-blower-motor

chapter 8

Troubleshooting 24-Volt Wiring Issues

Troubleshooting 24-volt wiring issues in HVAC systems is essential for maintaining reliable and efficient system operations. Technicians often encounter various challenges stemming from incorrect wiring connections, shorts, and other electrical problems that can cause erratic behavior or system failures. A systematic approach to diagnosing and resolving these issues not only ensures the HVAC system functions properly but also maximizes its lifespan and efficiency.

This chapter delves into specific methods for identifying and fixing shorts within a 24-volt HVAC system. It covers the step-by-step procedures for inspecting thermostat wiring, conducting continuity tests using a multimeter, and recognizing common symptoms of wiring faults. Additionally, it explores advanced diagnostic tools built into some thermostats and offers guidance on when professional assistance may be necessary. By following the detailed instructions provided, technicians will be equipped with the knowledge and skills needed to tackle 24volt wiring issues effectively and safely.

Dutch Pearson

Checking Wiring Shorts from

Thermostat

Many 24-volt HVAC wiring issues originate from the thermostat, making it vital to identify and resolve these problems. Thermostat wiring errors are common culprits behind various system malfunctions. Incorrectly connected wires can lead to several issues, such as erratic behavior or a complete lack of response. For instance, a technician may encounter a scenario where the heating system cycles unexpectedly or fails to turn on altogether. This often results from mixed-up or loose connections at the thermostat terminals. Therefore, a systematic approach to checking each wire's placement according to the manufacturer's specifications is fundamental.

To isolate problems in the wiring circuit effectively, using a multimeter for continuity testing proves invaluable. A multimeter helps determine whether a continuous electrical path exists within the wires, ensuring no breaks or faults. To conduct this test, first, disconnect the power supply to avoid any danger. Then, set the multimeter to the continuity mode and connect its probes to both ends of the wire in question. If the multimeter emits a beep or shows zero resistance, it indicates that the wire is intact. However, if there's no sound or the resistance is infinite, the wire is likely broken or damaged. Testing each wire individually helps pinpoint exactly where the fault lies, allowing technicians to address the issue efficiently.

Recognizing symptoms of thermostat shorts is another crucial aspect of troubleshooting. Typical symptoms include unexpected cycling of the HVAC system, which might result in uneven indoor temperatures. Another sign is the system's failure to respond to thermostat commands, leaving the space either too cold or too hot. Such behaviors are clear indicators of underlying wiring issues that need immediate attention. By understanding these symptoms, technicians can rapidly narrow down the potential causes, saving valuable time during diagnostics.

Implementing common troubleshooting steps further ensures comprehensive evaluation of thermostat wiring. Begin by switching off power to the HVAC system to maintain safety throughout the inspection process. Next, remove the thermostat cover and visually inspect the wiring connections, looking for any signs of corrosion, fraying, or loose wires. Tighten any loose connections and ensure all wires are secure in their respective terminals.

Following the visual inspection, use a multimeter to test each wire for continuity, as previously described. This step confirms whether the wires are in good condition or if they require replacement. Next, check the thermostat settings and calibration, ensuring it is not influenced by external factors like direct sunlight or drafts. Improper placement or calibration can lead to incorrect readings, causing the HVAC system to malfunction.

If the visual inspection and continuity testing do not reveal any issues, further probe into the control board connections where the thermostat wires terminate. Loose or corroded connections at this endpoint can also cause similar symptoms. By systematically checking these areas, one can verify the integrity of the entire wiring pathway from the thermostat to the control board.

Additionally, consider the possibility of interference from adjacent electrical devices. Electromagnetic interference can disrupt the signals between the thermostat and the control board, leading to erratic system behavior. Ensuring that low-voltage thermostat wires are properly shielded and routed away from high-voltage lines can mitigate this problem.

For more advanced diagnostics, some thermostats come equipped with built-in diagnostic tools. These tools can provide error codes or alerts indicating specific issues with the wiring or other components. Consulting the thermostat's user manual to interpret these codes can offer valuable insights and guide the troubleshooting process more accurately.

In cases where DIY troubleshooting does not resolve the issue, it may be necessary to seek professional assistance. Certified HVAC technicians have specialized equipment and expertise to handle complex wiring problems precisely. They can perform advanced tests, such as voltage drop analysis and signal integrity checks, which go beyond basic continuity testing. Engaging a professional helps prevent potential hazards and ensures the HVAC system operates safely and efficiently.

Testing Wiring Shorts from Air Handler to Condenser

Inspecting and resolving shorts between the air handler and condenser units in a 24-volt HVAC system is critical for maintaining system integrity. Technicians must be adept at identifying common points of failure along the wiring route, conducting voltage drop tests, utilizing visual inspections for wiring integrity, and implementing proper splicing techniques to ensure repairs are effective and safe.

One of the initial steps in troubleshooting shorts between the air handler and condenser is identifying common points of failure along the wiring route. These areas are typically prone to wear and potential damage due to various factors like vibration, moisture, and physical abrasion. Common points of failure often include connections at terminals, sharp bends in wiring, areas where wires pass through metal openings without grommets, and locations near moving parts. For instance, if wires are routed near fan blades or other rotating elements, the constant movement can eventually wear down the insulation, leading to shorts. Additionally, areas where wires are exposed to outdoor conditions may suffer from UV degradation or rodent damage. Highlighting these vulnerable spots allows technicians to focus their inspection efforts more effectively, thereby saving time and improving diagnostic accuracy.

Conducting voltage drop tests is another crucial technique for identifying wiring shorts and poor connections. Voltage drop occurs when there is resistance in the wiring, which can be a sign of a short or other connection issues. A significant voltage drop across a segment of wiring can indicate that the wire's integrity is compromised. To perform a voltage drop test, one should measure the voltage at two points along the circuit under load and compare the difference. A guideline here is to ensure that the voltage drop does not exceed 3% of the total circuit voltage. If the voltage drop is found to be higher than this threshold, it signals that the wiring needs closer inspection and possible repair. For example, if a technician measures a voltage drop of 1 volt in a 24volt circuit, it represents approximately 4.2%, which is above the acceptable limit and warrants further investigation.

Utilizing visual inspections for wiring integrity is essential for detecting abrasions or damage. Technicians should closely examine the wiring for signs of wear such as frayed insulation, discoloration, or cracks. It's important to look at areas where wires are in contact with other objects, such as metal edges or fasteners, which can cause abrasions over time. During the visual inspection, technicians should also check for signs of overheating, indicated by melted or scorched insulation. This visual assessment provides a quick and non-invasive method to identify potential issues before they escalate into more serious problems. Visual inspections should be part of regular maintenance routines to catch issues early and ensure ongoing system reliability.

Implementing proper splicing techniques is vital for ensuring any repairs to wiring are done effectively and safely. When a short is detected and a section of wiring needs replacement, the splicing method used can either uphold or compromise the integrity of the repair. Proper splicing involves stripping the wire ends to an appropriate length, twisting the exposed wires together firmly, and using suitable connectors such as wire nuts or crimp connectors. After making the connections, it's crucial to use heat shrink tubing or electrical tape to insulate the splice thoroughly. Guidelines for proper splicing techniques emphasize the importance of using materials rated for the specific voltage and environmental conditions of the installation. For example, if the splice is in an area exposed to moisture, waterproof connectors and sealants should be used to prevent future short circuits.

Core Message

In this chapter, we've explored essential techniques for identifying and resolving wiring shorts in 24-volt HVAC systems. From checking thermostat connections to inspecting the route from air handler to condenser, our focus has been on practical steps like continuity testing with a multimeter, visual inspections, and proper splicing methods. These approaches help ensure that technicians can diagnose and fix issues efficiently, maintaining the safety and reliability of HVAC systems.

Understanding common failure points and recognizing symptoms such as unexpected system cycling or non-responsiveness are critical skills for any HVAC technician. By applying systematic troubleshooting steps, including voltage drop tests and addressing potential interference, technicians can pinpoint and resolve shorts effectively. Equipped with these methods, you can enhance your ability to keep HVAC systems running smoothly, ensuring comfort and reliability for all users.

Reference List

4.4 Air Distribution System Ducts, Plenums, and Fans . (2016). Energycodeace.com. https://energycodeace.com/site/custom/public/referenceace-2016/Documents/44airdistributionsystemductsplenumsandfans.htm

Comfort, B. (2024, April 3). *Common HVAC Problems/How to Troubleshoot* . Dodrill Comfort & Energy Solutions. https://www.dodrillheating.com/blog/2024/april/common-hvac-problems-how-totroubleshoot/

Dutch Pearson

Furnace Circuit Board Troubleshooting: Identifying Faults & Solutions . (2024, September 9). Efficiency Heating & Cooling. https://www.eheatcool.com/services/heating/furnaces/furnace-repair/furnacecircuit-board-troubleshooting-identifying-faultssolutions/

chapter 9

Using cameras for heat exchanger inspection involves selecting the right equipment and setting it up correctly. The appropriate camera selection is critical, as different types of cameras such as thermal imaging cameras, borescopes, and high-resolution digital cameras serve specific purposes in HVAC inspections. Thermal imaging cameras help identify heat anomalies, while borescopes are useful for inspecting hard-to-reach internal parts, and high-resolution cameras provide detailed visuals of minor defects. Proper setup of these cameras involves adjusting focus, resolution, and exposure settings to ensure optimal image and video quality for thorough inspections.

The chapter will guide readers through the essential steps of preparing their cameras for effective heat exchanger inspections. It covers how to calibrate thermal cameras for accurate temperature readings and offers techniques for positioning cameras to access difficult areas. Readers will learn about using extendable poles, flexible borescopes, and robotic systems equipped with cameras to inspect intricate or hazardous spaces. Additionally, the chapter emphasizes the importance of recording and documenting inspection footage, using timestamped recordings, and organizing images and videos with dedicated software. This documentation process not only supports detailed evaluations but also ensures valuable records for future maintenance and audit purposes.

Setting up the camera for inspection

To equip readers with the knowledge necessary to prepare and position their cameras for optimal inspection results, ensuring comprehensive evaluations of heat exchangers, it is crucial to begin with understanding the appropriate camera selection. Different types of cameras are suitable for HVAC inspections based on their features, including thermal imaging cameras, borescopes, and high-resolution digital cameras. Thermal imaging cameras are particularly effective in identifying heat anomalies which can indicate potential leaks or inefficiencies. Borescopes, on the other hand, are invaluable for inspecting internal parts of heat exchangers that are difficult to reach or see directly. High-resolution digital cameras provide detailed visuals that help in identifying minute defects.

Once the appropriate camera type is selected, it is essential to set camera parameters to achieve the best video or image quality necessary for thorough inspections. This includes adjusting the focus to ensure clarity, setting the correct resolution to capture fine details, and configuring the proper exposure settings to handle variations in light within the environment. For thermal imaging cameras, calibrate the emissivity settings based on the material of the heat exchanger to get accurate temperature readings. Adjusting these parameters correctly ensures that any potential issues, such as heat spots or structural flaws, are clearly visible in the images or videos captured.

Positioning techniques are critical to accessing and inspecting hard-to-reach areas of heat exchangers effectively. Techniques include using extendable poles or flexible borescopes to navigate tight spaces and bends within the equipment. For instance, utilizing articulated borescopes allows technicians to maneuver around corners and obtain views from various angles. Implementing robotic systems equipped with cameras can also facilitate inspection in extremely confined or hazardous areas, providing a more comprehensive evaluation without exposing technicians to potential risks. Additionally, strategically positioning external lighting can enhance visibility in poorly lit sections, further aiding the inspection process.

Recording and documenting the inspection footage is equally important to ensure that all findings are properly archived and can be reviewed later for detailed analysis. Using timestamped recordings aids in tracking the timeline of inspections and correlating data with operational events. Employ dedicated software to organize and annotate images and videos, making it easier to reference specific issues at a later stage. Ensure that files are backed up in multiple locations, both physically and on cloud storage, to prevent data loss. Proper documentation practices not only support thorough evaluations but also provide valuable records for future maintenance and audit purposes.

Identifying common problems in heat exchangers

Recognizing and diagnosing various problems within heat exchangers is crucial for improving troubleshooting skills and ensuring the longevity and efficiency of these critical components. This segment will guide you through identifying signs of corrosion and wear, blockages and buildup, cracks and leaks, and overall efficiency evaluations using camera technology. Each aspect is essential for a thorough inspection and effective maintenance routine.

One of the first and most obvious signs that a heat exchanger may be experiencing issues is visible corrosion and wear. Corrosion occurs due to chemical reactions between the materials of the heat exchanger and the fluids it handles. Common indicators include rust, discoloration, and pitting on metal surfaces. During your inspection, focus on areas where moisture accumulates or where different metals come into contact, as these spots are particularly susceptible to electrolytic corrosion. Wear and tear can also manifest as thinning of the metal, which might not be immediately visible but can be detected using specialized camera equipment with appropriate magnification and lighting capabilities. Regular inspections for these signs can prevent minor problems from escalating into major failures.

Blockages and buildup within the heat exchanger pose another significant issue, leading to reduced efficiency and potential damage. Buildup can occur from sediment, scale, or biological growth within the tubes and passageways. Cameras equipped with flexible probes allow for a detailed internal view of these components. Look for narrowing passages, residue accumulation, or any obstructions that could impede fluid flow. Technologies such as infrared cameras can also detect temperature variations indicating clogs. Identifying these areas early enables targeted cleaning efforts, thus maintaining optimal heat transfer rates and prolonging the heat exchanger's lifespan.

Cracks and leaks are more severe issues that require immediate attention. Visual markers for cracks include irregular lines or streaks on metal surfaces, often running perpendicular to stress points or welds. Leaks can be identified by wet spots, drips, or corrosion patterns around joints and connectors. Using high-resolution cameras during inspections can highlight even minute hairline fractures that might be missed otherwise. Additionally, incorporating dye-penetrant testing during inspections can make cracks more visible. For leak detection, thermographic cameras are highly effective as they capture thermal anomalies caused by escaping fluids. Addressing cracks and leaks promptly prevents further degradation and ensures system integrity.

Evaluating the overall efficiency of heat exchangers is another key aspect of effective maintenance. Camera technology plays a significant role in these assessments by providing comprehensive visual data that helps evaluate the condition and performance of the heat exchanger. Efficiency can be compromised by several factors, including fouling, mechanical damage, and operational wear. During an inspection, use cameras to capture detailed images and videos of all accessible surfaces and internal structures. Compare current conditions with baseline images obtained when the equipment was new or last serviced. Discrepancies in surface appearance, such as increased roughness or uneven scaling, can indicate degrading efficiency.

In addition to visual inspections, cameras can assist in monitoring temperature distribution across the heat exchanger's surface. Infrared cameras, in particular, are valuable tools for this purpose. An even temperature distribution generally signifies good heat transfer efficiency, while hotspots or cold spots can indicate underlying issues like partial blockages or improper fluid flow. By regularly recording and analyzing this data, technicians can predict potential failures before they occur and schedule preventive maintenance accordingly.

Moreover, documenting the condition over time through recorded footage helps create a historical performance log, assisting in trend analysis and decision-making regarding repairs or replacements. This proactive approach ensures that heat exchangers operate at peak efficiency, thus saving energy costs and reducing downtime.

For example, in a scenario where a technician notices an upward trend in operating temperatures via infrared camera images, they might investigate further and discover a developing blockage. Early detection allows for the removal of the blockage using appropriate cleaning techniques, preventing a complete system shutdown. Similarly, discovering initial stages of corrosion can lead to implementing anti-corrosive treatments, extending the service life of the heat exchanger.

To wrap all these insights into your regular maintenance routine, start with a well-defined inspection process. Begin by capturing wide-angle shots of the heat exchanger's exterior for an overall condition assessment. Then, switch to closer inspections of critical areas like tube sheets, headers, and joints. Utilize both visible light and infrared cameras to cover all visual and thermal aspects comprehensively. Ensure that you follow safety protocols strictly, as working around heat exchangers often involves high temperatures and pressures.

Regularly updating your inspection techniques with advancements in camera technology can significantly enhance the accuracy and effectiveness of your assessments. Investing in training for technicians to proficiently use these tools is equally important. Proficient use of cameras not only aids in early problem detection but also provides clear evidence for making informed decisions about maintenance and repairs.

Final Thoughts

Throughout this chapter, we have explored the importance of selecting the right camera technology and properly setting it up for effective heat exchanger inspections. By choosing the appropriate types of cameras, such as thermal imaging cameras, borescopes, and high-resolution digital cameras, technicians can ensure comprehensive evaluations. Properly adjusting settings like focus, resolution, and exposure is critical to obtaining clear and useful images or videos. Additionally, techniques for positioning cameras in hard-to-reach areas using tools like articulated borescopes and robotic systems further enhance the inspection process.

We also delved into identifying common problems in heat exchangers, including corrosion, blockages, cracks, and leaks. Utilizing advanced camera technology aids in detecting these issues early, allowing for targeted maintenance and repairs. Regular documentation through recordings and proper organization ensures that findings are accessible for future reference and analysis. These practices not only help maintain the efficiency and longevity of heat exchangers but also contribute to safer operation and cost savings. Integrating these insights into a routine maintenance schedule enables

HVAC technicians to proactively address potential issues and keep systems running smoothly.

Reference List

A Step-by-Step Guide to Troubleshooting Your Heat Exchangers . (n.d.). https://www.maintwiz.com/troubleshooting-heat-exchangers-maintenancerepair-step-by-step-guide/

A Practical Guide to Machine Vision Lighting . (n.d.). Advanced Illumination. https://www.advancedillumination.com/a-practical-guideto-machine-vision-lighting/

Innasi Arokiasamy. (2024). *Heat Exchanger Inspection PDF* . Scribd. https://www.scribd.com/document/69641454/Heat-Exchanger-InspectionPDF

World, E. (2023, July 13). *Troubleshooting tips for tubular heat exchangers* . Heat Exchanger World.

https://heat-exchanger-world.com/troubleshootingtips-for-tubular-heat-exchangers/

chapter 10

Encourage Continuous Learning in the HVAC Field

Encouraging continuous learning in the HVAC field is essential for professionals who aim to remain at the forefront of their careers. The HVAC industry is continuously evolving, with new technologies and regulatory changes arriving each year. Staying updated on these advancements is not just an option but a necessity for anyone looking to provide efficient, eco-friendly solutions. By embracing a mindset of lifelong learning, HVAC professionals can ensure they are equipped to handle the dynamic nature of their work, whether it be through mastering smart thermostats, advanced diagnostic tools, or ecofriendly refrigerants.

In this chapter, we will delve into the various benefits that ongoing education brings to HVAC technicians. We'll explore how enhancing technical skills through continuous learning can lead to better job performance and increased customer satisfaction. Additionally, we'll examine the career advancement opportunities that come from staying knowledgeable about the latest trends and technologies. The chapter will also highlight how a commitment to learning fosters innovation and helps professionals navigate regulatory changes and product updates. Through practical examples and strategies, readers will be inspired to view this book as a starting point for their ongoing education and knowledge expansion in the HVAC industry.

The Importance of Continuous Learning in HVAC

Continuous learning is a fundamental pillar for HVAC professionals who wish to excel in their careers. The dynamic nature of the HVAC industry makes it imperative to stay abreast of evolving technologies and regulations. With each passing year, new advancements emerge, offering more efficient and environmentally friendly solutions. Whether it's the introduction of smart thermostats, advanced diagnostic tools, or eco-friendly refrigerants, the landscape of HVAC technology is ever-changing. As such, staying updated is not merely an option but a necessity.

One of the core benefits of ongoing education is the enhancement of technical skills. For HVAC professionals, proficiency in the latest technologies translates to better job performance. When you are adept at using the most recent tools and techniques, you can diagnose issues more accurately and solve problems more efficiently. This level of competence not only reduces downtime but also enhances overall customer satisfaction. Clients will appreciate the reduced waiting times and accurate fixes, which can lead to repeat business and referrals.

Moreover, continuous learning provides significant career advancement opportunities. In an industry where knowledge equates to power, staying knowledgeable keeps you competitive. Employers are continually on the lookout for individuals who can bring new insights and skills to their teams. By demonstrating expertise in the latest HVAC trends and technologies, you position yourself as a valuable asset. This proactive approach can lead to promotions, supervisory roles, or even specialized positions that come with higher earning potential. Additionally, certifications obtained through continuous learning can serve as formal recognition of your skills, making you more marketable in the job market.

Another essential aspect of continuous learning is the culture of innovation it fosters. HVAC professionals who engage in ongoing education are often more inclined to think outside the box and develop creative solutions to modern challenges. This innovative mindset is crucial, especially as the industry faces increasing demands for sustainability and energy efficiency. By staying educated, you open doors to pioneering methods and technologies that can solve emerging problems. Innovation driven by knowledge can lead to the development of new products or services that set you apart from competitors.

A practical example of this is the shift towards IoT (Internet of Things) in HVAC systems. Knowing how to integrate and maintain smart devices within HVAC setups requires continuous education. These smart systems can monitor energy usage, predict maintenance needs, and offer remote control capabilities, all of which contribute to more efficient operations and satisfied customers. Without continuous learning, HVAC professionals might miss out on the opportunity to leverage such transformative technologies.

Furthermore, regulatory changes are another critical reason for continuous learning. Governments and industry bodies regularly update codes and standards to ensure safety and environmental compliance. Being unaware of these changes can lead to costly fines, legal complications, or even endangerment of health and safety. Regular training ensures that HVAC professionals remain compliant with the latest regulations, thereby protecting both their businesses and their clients.

In addition to regulations, manufacturers frequently update product lines with new features and improvements. Staying informed about these updates allows HVAC professionals to recommend the best equipment to their clients. This knowledge ensures that installations are more reliable and efficient, leading to lower operational costs for customers and fewer callbacks for service technicians. It's a win-win scenario that stems directly from the commitment to continuous learning.

Strategies for Effective Continuous Learning

Engaging in continuous learning is crucial for HVAC professionals who want to stay competitive and effective in an ever-evolving industry. To ensure you are consistently growing your knowledge and skills, consider several practical methods that can be seamlessly integrated into your professional development routine.

One of the most effective ways to keep up with the latest advancements in HVAC technology and techniques is by utilizing online courses and webinars. Reputable organizations like ASHRAE (American Society of Heating, Refrigerating and AirConditioning Engineers) and ACCA (Air Conditioning Contractors of America) frequently offer these educational resources. Online courses provide flexibility, allowing you to learn at your own pace and on your schedule. Webinars, on the other hand, often feature live sessions where you can interact with instructors and peers, making them a great way to gain insights and ask questions about real-world applications. Embrace these digital learning platforms to stay informed about cutting-edge developments and best practices in the field.

Joining professional HVAC associations is another valuable strategy for continuous learning. Organizations such as the Refrigeration Service Engineers Society (RSES) and the Mechanical Contractors Association of America (MCAA) not only offer memberships but also host workshops, seminars, and conferences. These events are excellent opportunities for networking with fellow professionals, sharing experiences, and learning from experts. Participating in these gatherings can provide you with new perspectives and ideas that you can implement in your work. Additionally, many associations have local chapters, which means you can find relevant events close to home without needing extensive travel.

Reading industry publications and technical manuals regularly is an essential habit for staying updated. Magazines like *The NEWS* and journals from organizations like AHRI (Air-Conditioning, Heating, and Refrigeration Institute) are filled with articles detailing the latest trends, technologies, and regulatory updates. These resources often include case studies and expert opinions that can give you deeper insights into complex issues. Furthermore, technical manuals from equipment manufacturers can help you understand the intricacies of new tools and systems, ensuring you use them effectively and safely in your practice.

Investing time in hands-on training and certifications is equally important for mastering new tools, equipment, and techniques. Practical experience is invaluable in the HVAC field, where theoretical knowledge must be complemented by the ability to apply it effectively in various scenarios. Look for training programs that offer hands-on experiences, such as those provided by trade schools or manufacturers. Certifications from recognized bodies like NATE (North American Technician Excellence) or EPA (Environmental Protection Agency) not only validate your skills but also make you more marketable to employers and clients. These credentials demonstrate your commitment to excellence and your ability to handle complex tasks efficiently.

Final Thoughts

Continuous learning is essential for HVAC professionals to remain proficient and competitive in a rapidly evolving field. This chapter has highlighted the importance of staying updated with new technologies, enhancing technical skills, and keeping abreast of regulatory changes. By doing so, professionals can improve job performance, ensure client satisfaction, and position themselves for career advancement. The integration of innovative solutions such as IoT demonstrates how continuous learning can open doors to groundbreaking methods and more efficient operations.

It is crucial to view this book as a starting point for your ongoing education in the HVAC industry. Embrace available resources like online courses, professional associations, and industry publications to continually expand your knowledge. Hands-on training and certifications further validate your expertise and readiness to tackle new challenges. In an industry that values innovation and efficiency, your commitment to lifelong learning will set you apart and equip you to meet the future demands of the HVAC sector.

Biography

Christian Pearson, born in Magee, Mississippi, at 39 has spent much of his life moving between Mississippi, Texas, West Haven, Connecticut, and Colfax, California. With no GED, he has worked tirelessly in various roles, including the oil field and HVAC technician, mastering the trade from the ground up. He holds certifications in HVAC, heat exchangers, and LP gas, and Generac air and liquid cooled certified, served as a field support supervisor overseeing 25 technicians and as a field supervisor for five Generac technicians. His writing style is humorously informative, drawing life experiences to craft his narratives.